Waiting for the Southerly

Susan McCreery

Waiting for the Southerly

Acknowledgements

Poems in this collection have appeared in the following publications: *The Best Australian Poems 2009*, *Blue Dog*, *Dodecahedron*, *dotdotdash*, *Five Bells*, *FourW*, *Going Down Swinging*, *Hecate*, *Meuse Press*, *Poetrix*, *Tamba*, *The Memory Box*, *The Mozzie*, *Tide*, *Voices from the Meadow*.

Awards include First Prize Inverawe Nature Poetry Competition 2006 for 'Waiting for the Southerly'; Very Highly Commended 'Little Gems' Gemstones Literary Awards 2006 for 'Ruins'; Honourable Mention Inverawe Nature Poetry Competition 2008 for 'Eyrie'; First Prize All Poetry Competition 2009 for 'Head of the Table', Commended 2008 for 'Spider Wasp', Second Prize 2007 for 'Slippers'; Commended FAW (Eastwood/Hills) Literary Competition 2011 for 'Return to the Cyclades'.

Poems have been read at the Shoalhaven Poetry Festival 2007 and at the South Coast Writers Centre for National Poetry Week 2009. 'Split' was written in response to the Joan Meats painting *The Gatekeepers* and read at the Wollongong Art Gallery exhibition of Joan Meats' paintings 2008.

Thanks go to my writer friends Linda Godfrey, Elizabeth Hodgson, Andrea Gawthorne, Fay McDonald and Ali Jane Smith.

Waiting for the Southerly
ISBN 978 1 74027 732 7
Copyright © text Susan McCreery 2012
Cover photograph © Vincent Valle|Dreamstime.com
Author photograph by Scotti Hamilton

First published 2012
Reprinted 2016

GINNINDERRA PRESS
PO Box 3461 Port Adelaide SA 5015
www.ginninderrapress.com.au

Contents

Rock Fishing	7
Bone Dry	8
Hill	9
Inspection, 1965	10
Head of the Table	11
Alzheimer's	12
Wild Bird	13
Wanting	14
Slippers	15
Sea Dragon Dance	16
Spider Wasp	17
Foreign Harvest	18
Hooked on Greece	20
And It's Cold Down Here	21
Return to the Cyclades	22
Ruins	25
Split	26
Other Lovers	27
Waiting for the Southerly	28
Remnants	29
Wintering	30
Eyrie	31
Pathfinding	32
Rain at 4.30 a.m.	33
Spring	34
Autumn Waves	35
Reporting	36
Trial Bay, Winter	38
Easter Sunday	39
Due Date	40

'twas the rain	41
Impossible Blue	42
This House	43

Rock Fishing

for my mother

You used to fish off rocks
under whiskered cliffs
where crabs eyed me sideways
clicking like mice bones.

I watched your skill
with knife and knot,
your toughened skin
stained with gut.

I peered in pools
gummed with limpets,
anemones tugged my fingers
like blissful newborns.

We had the salt and wind,
the gulls poised on updraughts
and the far reach
from beach to open sea.

Now you cast
off weathered planks,
turn your eager eye
to the rocks, alert
for the sign of a taut line
a glittering catch, a run of kings.

Our reflections shudder
as the bait dances below.

Bone Dry

In a land as wide
as a drunken punch
cans lie glinting
like crooked cops.

A little boy
plays in the dust
apple shoulders scorched
by the sun.

Dad's on the fence
with a beer, piss-warm
from the clapped-out fridge.

The boy squints up
pleads for a drink
hands outstretched

like grubby stars
but the father's gaze
remains
on the far blue miles
and the crows
idling in for a kill.

Hill

Leave us on this
hill for a while this green
tumbling hill.

We promise to catch
up to the turning
earth
promise to make up time.

Palm fronds hang still
today
from sunlit spines.

We have
no appointments
let the earth move on
leave us
awhile.

Inspection, 1965

Your burnished shoes
are pressed as close
to clasping as feet can be.

He is the picture
of breakfast correctness
tie knot centred and tight

white shirt crisp
as an envelope.
You inhale the scent

of shaving soap,
wonder at his coppery hair
dark and weighted with oil.

At his nod of approval
your lips touch
his shower-moist cheek

and on the long path
to the bus stop
you break into a run

gathering armfuls of wind
satchel flying
shoes scuffed by stones.

Head of the Table

In the glare
of polite linen
he carves his words
with care
arranging them well
white black white.

You hide yours
under your tongue
swallow them whole
to dissolve
in your blood,
then pass the salt.

Once
you released them –
all ribbons
and colour, they shone
in the silver, trembling
with first-night nerves.

He took aim
fired, the thud went unheard
so close to your ribs.

You folded your napkin
straightened your knife
put away your boldness for years.

Alzheimer's

Has taken my father
To a place of circular walks,
Silent tea
And biscuits.

Has left my mother
Not widowed, but alone,
And his children
Visitors who help him
Sip from a cup
Find the toilet, then
Zip him up.

Turtle-like,
His head hangs,
Weary eyes blinking
At the grass, where I sit
Trying to catch words
That flit from his lips
Like moths,
Dusting the air
With traces of a man,
A manager of men, who

Sits on a bench
In a garden of circular walks,
Silent tea
And biscuits.

Wild Bird

My father stares at grass
the colour of weak tea.

Shadows circulate, as a cold
hand flexes the garden's joints.

Visitors come and go.

The eaves drip, drip
a solitary note on the mottled
moss of his mind

while onto his palm
the last familiar
face on earth places
a slice of lemon cake.

The day's thin eyelid
flickers at the brief
flare of a lorikeet.

Wanting

To save on shoe leather
my grandmother chose
grass verge over path.
My mother longed
for the shiny bugle
in the secondhand shop, pressing
nose to window on the way to school.
I tend my vegetables, wear
three-dollar skirts.
My children devour toy
catalogues – those lolly colours
preserved in gloss
undo all the old stories.

Slippers

her bunions
cushioned
in floss pink slippers
twilled with grime
shift over the lino
as he shambles in
to suck the hours
through his teeth
it's the sixth night in a row
she's cooked lamb chops
how long
before he notices?
small wars
small victories
she wears loss
& labour pinned to her chest
like a stuck heart
that night she stares
at the dark ceiling
as his dry hand
moves up her nightie
& onto her breast
fleur called today she says

Sea Dragon Dance

Below the surface
the sea pitters with life.
Two creatures draw close,

begin their mirror dance.
Fins fanning the current
they take turns to lead

and in the downward
drift of evening still they dance –
dipping their slender snouts

shimmying sideways –
until at last, above the dark
intimate sway of the weed bed,

rows of pink bubbles
latch to the male's sturdy tail
that will one day,

in the amniotic warmth
of a new season, hatch
hundreds of buoyant young.

Can you and I
learn to mirror dance
or would our leaden feet

take us down? If only
we could start again from here:
tiny, elegant, weightless.

Spider Wasp

Desperate for cover
legs working like frantic needles
antennae wired for danger

she drags the huntsman
up and down the summer
spikes of grass.

Her black abdomen, shot
with orange, shocks like the sight
of a mad nun

or a punk at a funeral.
Exposure is terrible.
For one risky moment

when a hefty bower bird
could blight her day
she leaves the dead

grey thing to scout the steps
hurries back, grasps it
vanishes

to reappear alone
on the wall behind the clivias, where
she stitches a nervous

cross-check over the bricks
before dropping to her hideout
under the dark straps of leaves.

Foreign Harvest

We truck-rattle
from the village to fields
of smoke-green leaves
on this white-breath
Cretan morning,
cast the first net
wide beneath a tree
and begin to beat
its branches, sending
black pellets flying.

Soon muscles warm
and stomachs groan
for morning tea –
raki and loukoumades
burn and sweeten
like turps with honey.

We move from tree to tree
each truant olive placed
in hessian sacks, not one
left to rot on the ground.

At midday
yia yia and her donkey
bring wine, bread
and horta doused in oil.
We sit on rugs
in stippled shade
before our afternoon attack.

Back in the village
it's been a good day's work.
I'm weary. I hear an old man
ask another who I am:
xeni,* but she hits well.
I'm proud, and for a moment
imagine I belong.

*xeni – foreigner

Hooked on Greece

I lie behind lashes,
amoebic, alert for footfalls.

Poacher-like, he moves
through angled shadows. Unseen,

I am reshaped by a fist.

Branded.

And sliced, swiftly as a pear,
juices coursing,
thrown up with the tide

and beached.

The night retreats
as the infant sun
creeps up the sheets
to his warm-armed curl
and nebulous breath, shifting
splinters in my idiot heart.

We sit enveloped in sunshine
at a small round table,
with eggs and Nescafé.

I think of my mother.

This week, my letter
will mention the spring
light on the Aegean.

And It's Cold Down Here

There were days, o
there were days
of rosewater skies
and the sea, thousands
of white pebbles
if you had carried me
if you had lain with me belly-close
in the wild thyme
moon over the water
benign, not taken
your fist to my face
not shocked a small purse
from my grasp
coins hard-pinging the floor
if winter had brought
breath-sleep folds
soft-cheek-loving
there might not be
this sound of metal
every time a hand
every time a smile
and it's cold down here
where only silent creatures walk
no one talks.

Return to the Cyclades

Easter

Sunset by the harbour we swing
our legs above water clear as air
as tavernas bubble with reunion.
Slim ribboned candles
dangle in shop windows, and
at midnight, when the deep
sky rejoices at the sound of bells,
strangers greet each other flame to flame.
At our table we lightly tap the gift
of three red eggs. My lamb
falls tenderly from its bones.

Roosters

How delightful if our ordered suburbs
held such an invitation to morning.
As I open blue shutters, the scent
of turned earth and olives in bud
enters the room with rooster crow.
The half moon pale as a veil
with night's withdrawal. Figs set
to burst like luscious vulvas.

Weddings

Borne along by jaunty bouzoukia
and a familial throng she arrives
at the pink pathway to the church.
Sparklers fizz, stars for the star,
and I wonder, will she end up
in fifty years time shuffling in black
weighed down with shopping
while the men walk so proud?

Myths

There's muscle to these mountains
their craggy peaks the thrusts of Dionysus.
I once ran wild like Ariadne, released
from ties, garlanded with poppies,
daisies, drunk on wine and love.

Evening

This is unchanged, how the cliffs
catch fire in the sun's soft fall,
how the sky, eggshell blue,
is as delicate as breath.
Dark ripples follow small boats
home to harbour and down on the paralia*
a man holds tight to his child's hand –
a stroll by the quiet water,
a kiss on the head, the flicker of swallows.
Now the sky's depth is violet,
endless, behind the blurred
heft of rock. A cat steps lightly
along the whitewashed rim of a stone wall.

*paralia – beach

Ruins

gangrenous, spittle-flecked sea
a disaster of sand, saddled
with weed, and your mouth
thin against the wind –
weekend carnage

Split

Written in response to the painting *The Gatekeepers* by Joan Meats (1920–2003)

How small I am
inching upwards
like a nail through mortar
here where it never rains.

There are no weeds
or rampant runners
no mad growth
only this sad wind.

Look how the road
curves like an arm
past the wordless gate.

I will travel at night
through this wild land.

You cannot embrace
in a cold house
however close you stand.

Other Lovers

shine in their skin – linked
christmas lights at midnight.

Meet in the kitchen
like pots of tea, warm and bellyful.

But we sit in this barren space,
this counselling room,
parched as bones on a gibber plain
picked at by scorpion malice,
and wonder how we came to roles
in such a worn-out play.

Other lovers
have a one-way flow,
their smiles flash
in the broad morning light.

We wake to a sickly dawn
and fear for our children.

Waiting for the Southerly

Blisters of sweat
sit between my breasts
as you and I watch our plates go dim
and mad mosquitoes jab
our heels through smoke
from red-tipped coils.

The escarpment shrinks
beneath a clotted fog
the house gags for breath
through fly screens –
we're sandbagged by February,
the butt end of summer.

In the bedrooms
small socks lie limp as tongues
pink feet twitch on cotton sheets
fans hum and click, and now,

blank as thumbnails,
we wait for distances of sleep,
sprawling towards our drop-offs
desperate not to touch.

Curtains pulse in the dark,
I glimpse a white-moon haze –

murraya flowers
gleam like pearls.

Remnants

Evening sneaks
into the neighbourhood
like a pale stranger,

subduing even the dogs.
A garage door
grates strips off the air.

At their father's,
the children have left
their remnants on the couch.

The egg water bubbles.
I watch a dark bird roller-coast
to a treetop, as a distant

piano fells my heart,
and imagine two small faces
lit against the sky.

Wintering

Today I woke to change,
the sea racing like a greyhound,
ears flattened, southerly
snapping at its heels.

I guessed it when my cold toes
intruded on my dreams,
when the skateboard took the wind
for a ride and the canvas chairs set sail.

Tonight an icy membrane of glass
is the thin wall of my cave
I draw the curtains early
despite the sky, delicate
as a blue egg, despite the white-lipped sea.

I need this bunkering down
it's been a talkative summer
the pantry's stocked
the grass slow-growing
I won't see much of the neighbours till spring.

In the radiator's red glow
I curl and slumber.

Eyrie

From my eyrie
light can be glitter,
or hammered flat and bright.

Sometimes rain roars up from the south,
or hangs off leaves,
cliffs blotched with fog.

Sometimes the sea
is as grey as habit,
or a hip-swinging blue.

Sometimes there's nothing
between me and the clouds
the rooftops wear.

Then last night I met you,
the blue of your eyes
gracing the lean shadows of your face.

Your sinewy hands
could shield an egg
from a gale, or fry one.

Tracks around your mouth
show that laughter
plays there frequently.

Since last night I've been thinking:
Is it time to step out
of my nest of skin,

is it time to let the weather in?
Since seeing you
am I done with the view?

Pathfinding

Not one whizzing cyclist's bell on this long coastal path
as I try to outpace thought. No walkers either – perhaps they're indoors

living usefully. A coterie of gazanias on the verge
toss their sunny heads at me – the odd one out.

Squat shrubs, arthritic from the sea's shifting vapours,
shiver as I pass. Like walking off a rich dessert

I walk off you. Love is dense with calories – each step burns.
Dependable arrows guard against disarray.

'Pathfinders', those monster off-roaders,
have no place here, it is for foot traffic and clean wheels only.

I think of goats and shepherds, of well-trodden tracks,
sodden stretches of heath and marsh, familiar only to locals.

This path is my familiar. Time to click my heels and return.
I believe twenty minutes is good enough for the heart.

Rain at 4.30 a.m.

Cold on my shoulders.
The gusting rain has lowered
the temperature of the window.
Something has brought me
into complete wakefulness.
I lean down for a book,
leaf through Mary Oliver,
shed tears for her dead uncle,
her muddy father.
Lightning and growl
of thunder. What else
to do at this solitary hour?
The children sleep. Will I
before they wake? I make
plans. Recite poems. The wild
rain has steadied. Today we won't
walk to school. The snails must be
feasting on my tender
vegetables. My shoulders
are cold. Last night
so hot I tossed irritably.
I must empty the gutters of leaves.
I must wrap a present. I must swim.
I must write. I must lose
another inch from my waist.
I don't know if I will sleep.
But I have listened to the rain.
And I have written.

Spring

fireflies dance
on the ocean at noon,
the breeze, too,
wants to dance
under a generous sun,
me in its arms,
after days
of grey thoughts

the earth-warmed air
streams into my lungs
and neighbours
bring their tables outside –

in their voices
I can almost hear flutes

Autumn Waves

You raced for the autumn sea
leaving me to my warm hollow
of sand to hail each wave
you caught, and when I tried to sneak
a look at the sky that was like a note
from a violin, so pure it hurt,
your call recalled my eyes
and I thought: there'll always be skies like this
but your small face, frilled
by froth, may never gleam
as bright as it does today
as you tumble towards the shore and me.

Reporting

October seems confused,
we shed clothes
put them on, look
to the sky for clues
shake our heads.

Last week the relentless
smack of blowflies
on glass, shut
against the sun
later flung wide
for any chance cool.

Next day heaters
retrieved from storage
as snow falls
in Katoomba.

At night the news
is complicated
people run with their money
presidents race to the finish line.

I've heard the Japanese
report on blossoms
no matter what.

Our jacarandas
I'd like to report
are quietly blooming,
each bell's tentative swell
soon to unite
in a wild mauve
ringing-in-the-summer.

And the flame trees,
daily I rake the clumsy leaves,
above me a slow
burn to blaze.

My winter skin
will sing
when I finally take the plunge
the cold sea.

Trial Bay, Winter

Star light, star bright,
First star I see tonight,
I wish I may, I wish I might,
Have the wish I wish tonight.

          19th-century nursery rhyme

Shadow puppets, the children play tip,
their calls weaving through dusk
like silver ribbons.

Across the bay
mountains ink themselves
onto the sun's final flush of colour.

Venus rises – star of the sea –
as if the sky, scooping to drink,
had found a jewel and put it on.

The water is strewn with wedding rings.
The children say the magic rhyme,
I know all I wish is here.

The sand, and their feet at play
are the last pale things
in a landscape of dark shapes.

Easter Sunday

I took my boy to church,
thinking he should at least
have the opportunity –
he likes scripture at school.

Outsiders without words
we sat together on the pew
he, quite still
with trembling chin
and brimming tears
as with a surge
they surged to sing
hallelujah! to guitar and drum.
I didn't know whether to laugh or cry.

Children gathered at the front
knew all the answers to the Easter questions
clustered round a giant egg.

He sat by me.

Back home
we stripped off our Sunday best
rolled on the grass
the autumn sun dancing
on leaves, on me, on him

free of the hymning, humming, mouthing
stand up/sit downs
and all those welcoming smiles
circling us – a net
of good intentions
side-stepped as we left.

Due Date

Unusual, the blinds are up
at nightfall, the house
a dazzle of light.

Grandpa stands centre-rug
a maypole, ringed by two prancing
wet-haired girls in PJs
while grandma busies cushions on the couch.

No sign of mum or dad –
right at this moment
she might be in a mid-birth
haunch, flanked by him
and the midwife.

There's nothing like waiting for a baby
nothing like the drawing in
the mustering of relatives
the pent air.

Looking out from my darkened window
looking in on this world
I remember a time when
I, too, was a woman
time stopped for.

'twas the rain

i'm breathing *rain*
on hot pillows of air
damp roads steam
under wheels, fungal feet
squished into sandals
slide over footpaths like slugs
into reject shop aisles where shoppers
push sideways spending more & more
on last-minute breakable lurid trash, like this spray-
painted dragon whose crimson gemstone
will tumble out on boxing day like a glass eye,
like this box of sugar-coated santas
on sticks, like these dvds to watch in
the *rain*, like these socks with snowflakes
never to be worn *again*, while assistants
nod their antlers smile their christmas
cheer & office workers spill out
like *beer*, boozed up & cackling
in these scrambled cicada-drumming days
as we tick off gifts & i can't walk
in a straight
                       line because everyone seems mad
hopelessly lost in the *rain*

Impossible Blue

(after Haiti earthquake, 2010)

Half past five
the sand surrenders its heat
the length of the beach a ruin
of prints, hollows and mounds.

As I spread my towel
families shake, fold, pack,
turning from the solace
the cool of the sea.

This is the in-between time
that lull in the day
when a raised hand
suspends the digging.
I listen to the dozing waves.

And how is the sky to a boy
after eight days' darkness,
how is the sky
this impossible blue?

This hue, the waves, that brown girl
in a bubblegum suit
and all along the sand
dried clumps of weed
like hundreds of corpses
waiting, waiting.

This House

Our night-breath
wreathes
room to room

spun together
we're impervious
to weather

even the pesky mynahs
lie low outside
our lamplit home.

I have shored us up –
an old-growth mother
sunk deep in wormy soil

dangerous with history
but green
dew green.

The wind kicks black glass
the street tree rubs
its coin of light.

www.ingramcontent.com/pod-product-compliance
Lightning Source LLC
Chambersburg PA
CBHW062207100526
44589CB00014B/1987